Lion
Journal
By
Carolyn Fran[klin]

Note to the reader.
This book is a fictional
account of a safari in the
Masai Mara, Kenya. It is based
on a series of separate
experiences that have been
adapted to fit the storyline.

A weaver bird's nest

1 3 5 7 9 8 6 4 2

A CIP catalogue record for this book is available from the British Library.

HB ISBN-13: 978-1-906370-58-9
PB ISBN-13: 978-1-906370-60-2

Printed and bound in China.
Printed on paper from sustainable sources.

Visit our website at www.salariya.com
for **free** electronic versions of:
You Wouldn't Want to be an Egyptian Mummy!
You Wouldn't Want to be a Roman Gladiator!
Avoid Joining Shackleton's Polar Expedition!
Avoid Sailing on a 19th-Century Whaling Ship!

PUBLISHED BY BOOK HOUSE 25 MARLBOROUGH PLACE, BRIGHTON

Consultant: John Cooper

Photo credits:
Dreamstime, Fotolia, iStockphoto,
Jonathan Salariya

Published in Great Britain in 2009
by
Book House, an imprint of
The Salariya Book Company Ltd,
25 Marlborough Place, Brighton,
BNI IUB
www.salariya.com
www.book-house.co.uk

PAPER FROM
SUSTAINABLE
FORESTS

A curious giraffe!

Contents

YOR
8/09

Lioness and her cubs

ippo in a hurry!

What to take

For as long as I can remember I have dreamt of seeing lions in the wild. I have spent the last year planning my trip. Tomorrow I'll fly to Kenya in East Africa. The lions I am going to visit live in the Masai Mara Game Reserve near Kenya's border with Tanzania.

CHECK LIST:
Passport and visa
Flight tickets
Medication
Maps and directions
Local money
Note book
Vaccination cert.

Preparation:
Check doctor for injections/tablets required (for protection against tsetse flies and mosquitoes!) The planes will be small, so travel light. Take minimum of luggage in small (soft) kit bag.

AFRICA
Kenya

Map of the
Masai Mara

KENYA

Oloololo Gate
Mara River
Musiara Swamp
To Ationg
To Nairobi, Siana Springs
Talek Gate
Euai Plain
Sekenani Gate
Kurao Plain
The Mara Triangle
Olempito Hill
Mara Wildlife Research Station
To Narok
Ololamutiek Gate
Mara Bridge
Sand River Gate

Serengeti National Park

TANZANIA

ETHIOPIA

Lotikipi Plain
Lake Turkana
Sibiloi National Park
Loima Hills
Moyale
Mandera
NDA
South Turkana National Reserve
Marsabit National Reserve
Kitale
Losai National Reserve
KENYA
SO
Kisumu
Meru Nat. Park
Mt. Kenya Nat. Park
Mount Kenya
*Naivasha
Masai Mara Game Reserve
Garissa
Nairobi
Arawale Nat. Reserve
Serengeti National Park
Amboseli
Tana River Primate Nat. Reserve
Ngorongoro Crater
Mount Kilimanjaro
ANZANIA
INDIAN OCEAN
Shimba Hills Nat. Park
Mombasa
Pemba Island

4

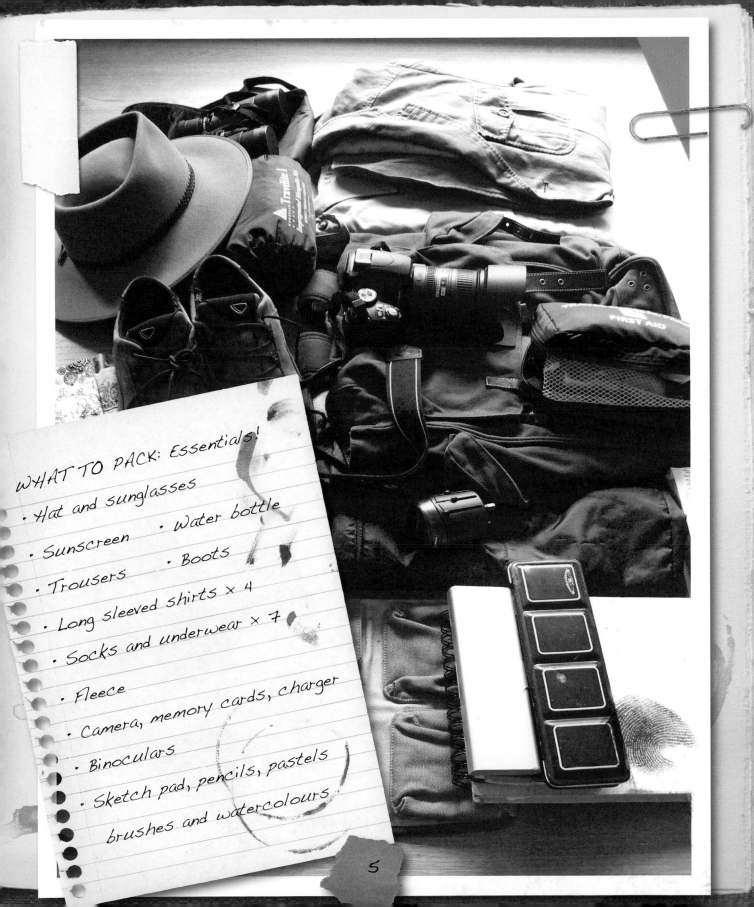

WHAT TO PACK: Essentials!

- Hat and sunglasses
- Sunscreen   · Water bottle
- Trousers   · Boots
- Long sleeved shirts × 4
- Socks and underwear × 7

- Fleece
- Camera, memory cards, charger
- Binoculars
- Sketch pad, pencils, pastels
  brushes and watercolours

The word **Mara** means 'spotted' which refers to the thorny acacia trees that are dotted over the landscape.

Time to go!

Monday 12th August
10 AM: boarding aircraft

I arrived in Kenya yesterday. Now it's 10 AM and the group I am travelling with are about to board a small plane to fly to Naivasha. From there we will drive overland to the Masai Mara. The Mara is Africa's largest game reserve and covers nearly 1,500 square kilometres of savannah grassland.

The Masai Mara

The Masai Mara Game Reserve is in south-west Kenya. It's an ideal destination for seeing lions. Its rivers never dry up so they provide a continuous water supply for huge numbers of wild animals. The forest areas beside the Mara River support elephants and giraffes and the huge plains attract lions, cheetahs, leopards, hyenas, jackals and many other animals.

Acacia trees on the Masai Mara

12 AM: Meet guide

Our guide's name is Wambua which means 'born in the rainy season'. His family come from this area so he's a real local!

Wambua asks us to keep with him at all times and not to forget that the animals are wild and can be very dangerous. He also told us not to leave things lying around especially at camp, because monkeys will steal anything!

A group of hippos is called a herd!

I was amazed to learn that hippos are one of the most feared animals in Africa! Hippos have attacked people who get between them and the water. Apparently, more people are killed each year by hippos than by any other African animal. It's hard to believe!

I almost missed seeing this crocodile. It was on the bank, under some bushes but it was as still as a statue.

Arriving at camp

Earlier we crossed the Mara River by boat. We saw crocodiles resting on the river bank and a herd of hippos that plunged into the water as we approached. Wambua told us that during the day hippos keep cool by wallowing in mud or relaxing in the river. At dusk they leave the river to graze on the grass.

After a short trek through the forest we arrived at the campsite. We've arranged our tents near a waterhole. I am amazed at how many birds there are - they seem to be everywhere. Wambua says that giraffes, elephants, zebras, hippos and warthogs all come here to drink and graze.

Our campsite

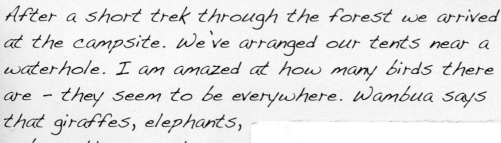

Bush baby!

Last night I was so excited that I barely slept. Just before daybreak I heard noises and peeked out of my tent. Just outside were two bush babies! One had got its head stuck inside a glass and wobbled the table so much that it fell over, sending both bush babies and the glass crashing to the ground! The commotion sent them fleeing into the bush!

Grasshopper on my hand!

Tuesday 13th August

A young male
and female lion

Acacia thorn
bush

First sighting

The sun is rising over the Masai Mara as we set off for our first early morning game drive. We are all excited. We drive in silence for about 20 minutes until the jeep slows down and Wambua points! There, just in front of us, are two lions lying in the grass, a male and female (or lioness). Wambua says they are about two years old. They are quite relaxed and more or less ignore us as we lean out of our jeep, frantically taking photographs.

Wambua sees more lions in the distance and we set off towards them. Our jeep approaches slowly and we stop far enough away so we do not disturb them but close enough to see them clearly.

Bumpy ride in the jeep

Heading back to camp for breakfast we pass this buffalo skull!

In the heat of the day, most animals rest. They are more likely to be seen in the early morning or late afternoon. Wambua tells us that female lions do most of the hunting.

A lioness enjoys a meal

Tuesday 13th August

Close encounter

It's late afternoon and we're off in the jeep again. Wambua spots a lion kill (a zebra) and drives us closer. I cannot believe our luck – a mother and cub are feeding on the zebra. The cub is copying its mother, trying to learn how to eat such a large animal!

Her cub soon joins her

The cub practises its pounce!

At a kill it is normal for the adult lions to eat first. Sometimes a male will take the prey for himself, and the cubs have to wait their turn to eat whatever is left. When prey is scarce, the cubs get very little food and they can die of starvation.

Back at camp...

This is the best day of my life! We have already seen more lions than I had ever imagined possible and it's only our first day. The monkeys scatter as we return to camp but we've had another visitor too - there is a fresh lion footprint less than 10 metres from my tent!

Lion footprint near tent!

A hairy caterpillar - I found it under my bed

The savannah

Thanks to its colouring, a lion is camouflaged against the tall yellow-brown savannah grasses. This makes it difficult for us to spot them. Lions' prey can also be hard to see. Surprisingly, zebra markings act as camouflage too. Wambua told us that lions are colour-blind so a zebra's black and white stripes can look like a patch of grass to a hungry lion.

Wednesday 14th August 6 AM

It's early morning, yet the savannah is incredibly hot. I am glad I wore my hat and sunglasses! It's the middle of the dry season - the grasses look almost dead.

SPOTTER'S GUIDE
Animals of The Savannah

Cheetah

Weight: Males 900-1,400kg
Height: 1.6-1.7m
Length: 3.2-3.4m, plus tail: 70cm
Lifespan: 30-40 years

Weight: Males 41-57kg
          Females 36-45kg
Height: 70-80cm
Length: 1.2-1.4m,
          plus tail: 60-80cm
Lifespan: about 10 years

Rhinoceros

Cape buffalo

Elephant and calf

Weight: Males 500-800kg
          Females 550kg
Height: 1.4-1.6m
Length: 1.8-2.5m,
          plus tail: 60-70cm
Lifespan: 15-20 years

Weight: Males 5,000-6,000kg
          Females 2,750-3,250kg
Height: Normally 2.7-3.2m,
          can be up to 4m
Lifespan: about 60 years

So far I've seen:

Lions, cheetahs, rhinoceroses, elephants, water buffaloes, giraffes, hippos, hyenas, ostriches, zebras, elands, impalas, wildebeest, warthogs and baboons.

A typical Masai home

Wambua took us to visit a Masai village. The Masai women build the houses out of branches, twigs and grass bound together by cow dung.

Masai villagers

The Masai people are mainly cattle and goat herders. Nowadays they supplement their income by selling beads, masks and carvings to tourists. I bought a beautiful wooden lion.

Grasses from the savannah

Only male lions grow manes – the long hair around their face that covers their head, neck and shoulders. Wambua told us that the manes of Masai Mara lions are often darker than lions from other parts of Africa.

Wednesday 14th August (mid-afternoon)

Family groups

Lions are the only cats that live in family groups, called prides. A pride can include up to three males, twelve or more females and their young.

A pride relaxing in the shade

The heat is overwhelming. I can understand why lions need to rest in the shade during the hottest part of the day.

The females in a family group are almost always related - perhaps sisters or cousins. They help one another to look after all the cubs, not just their own.

A female will raise her tail as a 'follow me' signal for the cubs.

Mothers and cubs

The lionesses in a pride generally give birth at about the same time. When a lioness is ready, she finds a sheltered spot away from the pride where she gives birth to between 2 and 6 cubs. Newborn cubs are vulnerable and may fall prey to hyenas or other predators when the lioness leaves them to go hunting.

A lioness carrying her cub

If a lioness is worried about her cubs' safety, she will carry them in her mouth, one by one, to a new hiding place.

Grooming!

Lions have rough tongues which help to get insects out of each others' fur when grooming.

6.30: This lioness and her family are drinking at a waterhole. Wambua says that they have probably just eaten, since lions normally only drink to help digest food.

6.30 PM: At the waterhole

This cub must be full!

Lion cubs

When lion cubs are born they have a slightly spotted coat which becomes the same colour as their parents after about three months. When the cubs are big enough to follow her, the lioness takes them to the pride to introduce them to their father. This can be a dangerous time as a male lion will sometimes kill the cubs and their mother, if she tries to defend her young. Young cubs may suckle from other lionesses in the pride as well as from their own mother.

Spots make good camouflage!

Thursday 15th August
(near the River Mara)

Cubs at play

We had great fun watching two cubs stalking each other and play-fighting. This kind of play is important as it helps the cubs to learn hunting skills.

Wambua says that by about 3 years of age, young male lions must leave their pride. Those males born around the same time will usually stay together for the rest of their lives. When they are older and fully grown, they will take over another pride, replacing a dominant male that has become too old or weak. When this happens they sometimes kill all the existing cubs.

Lion's prey

Zebra

Buffalo

Warthog

Wildebeest

Impala

Female lions do most of the hunting, mainly at night, late afternoon or in the early morning.

We actually saw a kill today. It was astonishing to watch the lionesses in action, but shocking too. Wambua has even seen lions attacking a crocodile!

Thursday 15th August (late afternoon)

Hunting

A lion's prey includes wildebeest, zebra, waterbuck, giraffe, kudu and buffalo. A lion will get as close as possible to its prey by hiding in the grasses and slowly creeping up until the prey is about 20 to 30 metres away. Then it will charge its unwary prey. Old, sick or injured animals make easy targets.

Three lionesses attacking a young buffalo

22

Lionesses work together to stalk and ambush their prey. This quick sketch shows three lionesses waiting downwind of a zebra herd so the zebra cannot smell them. The fourth lioness moves upwind of them. Suddenly she dashes out, chasing the zebra herd towards the others that lie in wait.

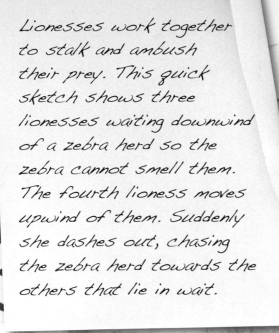

Direction of wind

Chases zebra

Startled herd of zebra

Vultures - always on the look-out!

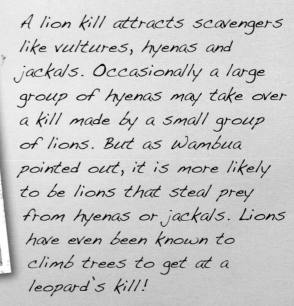

A lion kill attracts scavengers like vultures, hyenas and jackals. Occasionally a large group of hyenas may take over a kill made by a small group of lions. But as Wambua pointed out, it is more likely to be lions that steal prey from hyenas or jackals. Lions have even been known to climb trees to get at a leopard's kill!

23

A lion's roar is louder and deeper than a lioness's and can be heard up to 8 kilometres away! Wambua says that it's magnificent to hear lions roaring together! I would love to hear that.

Friday 16th August very early...

Lion behaviour

A lion pride will defend its territory against other lions. They identify their territory by loud roaring, by spraying trees and rocks with urine and by scuff marking. Wambua points out claw marks on a tree where the lions have been scratching (or scuff marking). Lions also roar to communicate with the rest of the pride or to show anger towards an unknown lion.

Friday 16th August
much later...

Affectionate lions

Friday 16th August

It is late afternoon and we're on the road again. Wambua's alert eyes are constantly searching. He pulls up and points to a group of lions that none of us has spotted. Spellbound, we watch through our binoculars: an adult male and female are resting their heads on the back of a young male lion.

At their feet three cubs snuggle up to their mother. I asked Wambua if this affectionate behaviour is common. Apparently, a pride of lions will touch each other in greeting, and when resting they rub heads, lick and purr.

Lion habitat

African lions don't live in dense forests and jungles, or in desert areas where there is hardly any game. They prefer to live in open plains like the Mara where there is a permanent water supply and plenty of grass which attracts lots of animals for them to hunt.

Sunset over the Masai Mara

Saturday 17th August
...my last evening

The best time to visit the Masai Mara is in the dry season, from July to October, when the grass is long and lush after the rains. There are vast herds of zebra, impala and wildebeest. I came here to see lions, but I've seen much more: elephants, rhinos, buffaloes and even a leopard!

Impala and zebra grazing together

We have been following the same pride for two days now. Wambua has names for each lion and explained how he identifies individual lions. I quickly sketched a male lion known as 'Jomo' to show the features that make him identifiable.

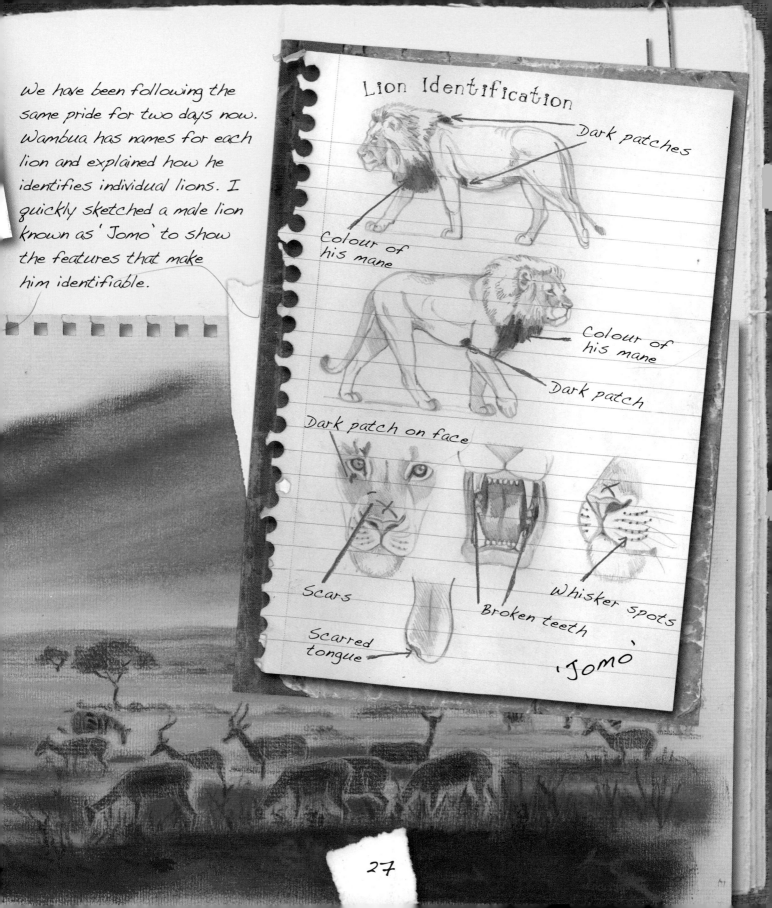

Lion Identification

Dark patches

Colour of his mane

Colour of his mane

Dark patch

Dark patch on face

Scars

Scarred tongue

Broken teeth

Whisker spots

'Jomo'

GLOBAL WARMING

Scientists have linked climate shifts in East Africa to major declines in lion populations in 1994 and 2001. These two tragic periods were preceded by extreme droughts. Lack of rain caused the savannah grasslands to dry up. Weakened by lack of food, the lions' prey became infected by disease-carrying ticks. The lions feasted on the prey and were themselves infected, leading to many disease-related deaths.

Fewer than 3,000 lions are left in Kenya

Are lions in danger?

Africa's lions are in danger. They used to be all over Africa but now they are only found in the south Sahara desert and in parts of southern and eastern Africa. Lions need huge areas to hunt in, but as people take over more and more of the remaining wild areas for farming, lions are being forced into smaller and smaller territories.

Lions are also under threat from diseases such as animal tuberculosis and canine distemper that can be spread by cattle and dogs.

When lions live near farmland they are often shot, caught in snares or poisoned because they are seen as a danger to the farm animals.

28

I learned from Wambua that lions are still hunted for sport. He explained that certain African governments encourage hunting as it brings in an income for some of the poorer countries. It gives the local people a reason to conserve the lions, since their presence will attract wealthy hunters.

Ooh! These lion skins were at a local market

HUNTERS
Threaten Africa's lions

Rich trophy-hunters who pay thousands of pounds to shoot big game in fenced enclosures are big business in Africa. The price of shooting a lion bred in captivity ranges from about £9,000 to £16,000, and the breeders who supply the trade are struggling to keep up with demand. While some estimates suggest that there are less than 20,000 wild lions remaining in rica, the International Fund for imal Welfare reports that another 0 languish in captivity, bred as ets for trophy-hunters. E

Spokesperson for the l

Deadly virus attacks African lions

Tourists were the first to notice that the lions were sick. In 1994, they were taking a balloo

Lion numbers down due to loss of habitat

What can we do?

Wambua told us that governments are at last becoming much more aware of the importance of lions - not only as part of African culture, but as a major tourist attraction. Illegal poaching has to be stopped and legal hunting must be monitored. Lions need protection and enough land to allow their numbers to increase if the species is to survive.

Governments pull together to save lions

Governments, biologists and other professionals decide to focus on making policies for land use that reduces human–lion conflict. The illegal trade in lions and lion products must be banned, and lion conservation is to become high priority. For conservation to succeed, wildlife has to pay for itself in Africa. Permits allowing selective hunting have already proven to be effective, encouraging landown... and provide l...

Note: Must check out organisations such as The African Lion Working Group – www.african-lion.org

Wambua says the best way we can help lions is to tell people about their plight. If enough people care, governments will continue to protect both the lions and the areas of savannah where they live.

Words to remember

Camouflage The markings and colourings on an animal's coat that allow it to blend in with its surroundings.

Downwind When the wind direction blows the scent of an object or animal away from it. Lions stand downwind of their prey so that the prey will not detect the lions' scent.

Eland Huge African antelope with long, spiralling horns and thin vertical stripes/markings.

Game reserve An area of land set aside for wildlife to allow it to thrive.

Grazing Feeding on plants such as grasses.

Habitat The place in which a plant or animal naturally belongs.

Mammal A warm-blooded animal which has hair or fur. Female mammals produce milk to feed their young.

Poaching The illegal practice of killing animals for meat, skins, ivory or trophies.

Pride A group of lions.

Savannah A large, grassy plain, often dotted with trees.

Scavenger An animal that feeds on other dead animals.

Stalking Hunting prey by moving silently and stealthily towards it or by waiting in ambush.

Suckling When a mammal feeds her young with her own milk.

Territory The area that an animal defends against intruders of its own species.

Index